W. W. Howe

Kinston, Whitehall and Goldsboro (North Carolina) expedition, December, 1862

W. W. Howe

Kinston, Whitehall and Goldsboro (North Carolina) expedition, December, 1862

ISBN/EAN: 9783337056988

Printed in Europe, USA, Canada, Australia, Japan

Cover: Foto ©Andreas Hilbeck / pixelio.de

More available books at **www.hansebooks.com**

KINSTON,

WHITEHALL AND GOLDSBORO

(NORTH CAROLINA)

EXPEDITION,

December, 1862.

NEW YORK,
W. W. HOWE,
157 E. 37TH STREET,
1890.

Copyrighted by
W. W Howe, New York City,
1890.

To the

MOTHERS

WHO WERE EVER THOUGHTFUL OF THEIR
ABSENT ONES, AND TO THOSE

COMRADES

WHO ANSWERED THE LAST CALL
AND HAVE PASSED TO THE OTHER SIDE, ALSO TO MY

COMRADES

WHO HAVE BEEN LEFT BEHIND TO FIGHT
THE BATTLE OF LIFE,

THIS LITTLE MEMENTO,

IS RESPECTFULLY DEDICATED, WITH THE HOPE
THAT THE MEMORIES IT WILL REVIVE
WILL SERVE TO UNITE US AS STRONGLY IN THE FUTURE
AS IN THOSE DAYS OF

"'62."

PREFACE.

The letter press from New York Herald, Dec. 20-25, 1862, by permission, also New York Times. The illustrations of Kinston, Whitehall and Goldsboro, also portrait of Gen. J. G Foster, are reproduced from Harper's History of the Rebellion, by arrangement with Messrs. Harpers Brothers.

New York, Dec. 1, 1890.

CONTENTS.

Commencement of the March, ... 9
Battle of Kinston, ... 14
Battle of Whitehall, ... 16
Battle of Goldsboro, ... 17
Death of Colonel C. O. Grey, ... 58
Losses in the Three Battles, ... 77
Death of Major General John G. Foster, . . . 82
Obsequies of Major General John G. Foster, . . 86
List of Regiments in the Expedition, ... 89
Index, ... 93

KINSTON, WHITEHALL, GOLDSBORO

NORTH CAROLINA.

Expedition, December, 1862.

In the Field, Fifteen Miles from
New Berne, Dec. 11, 1862.

Major General J. G. Foster commenced a movement of his army from New Berne this morning. At 3 p. m. we came upon the enemy's pickets (near our present camping ground), when three prisoners were taken by the advance guard of the Third New York Cavalry. In attempting to press forward we found the road densely blockaded by felled trees; this blockade extended for several hundred yards, being situated in the midst of a swamp possessing an abundance of creeks. Owing to this obstruction it became absolutely necessary to halt here for the night. During the same time the woods were cleared and with great rapidity, too, by pioneers from several regiments and a strong force of "pioneer contrabands"—the latter under the direction of the civil engineer of this department, Henry W. Wilson.

DECEMBER 12, 1862.

During the past night the Ninth New Jersey Infantry, under command of Colonel Heckmann, advanced through the swamp and took up a position within three miles of Trenton, engaging the enemy successfully for a short time.

At 9.30 o'clock to-day we came upon a body of rebel cavalry and an ambush of rebel infantry. Captain Marshall, with Company B., of the Third New York Cavalry, charged the enemy's cavalry, driving them ahead, taking seven prisoners and wounding or killing the captain of the company, besides killing and wounding a few others. In this charge we lost four men, who were taken prisoners; also Franklin Kingsley, who was wounded in the leg, and Augustus G. Butler, who was wounded in the side. We had other light skirmishing during the day; also took a few more prisoners.

DECEMBER 13, 1862.

We advanced at daylight, making several feints on various roads, but always finding the enemy posted in such a manner as to be able to destroy the bridges and otherwise retarding our movements. About 9 o'clock, Company K., Captain Cole, of the Third New York Cavalry, came upon the enemy at a place called Southwest Creek. The rebels had an earthwork thrown up directly across the road. Behind it they had posted four guns. Captain Cole attempted to charge across the bridge, but found it partially destroyed. He then retired a short distance, after leaving John Costello wounded in the face, when the rebels opened fire with their artillery and small arms. We returned the fire with carbines, driving the enemy for several minutes from a piece of his artillery, which was posted at the other end of the bridge. About this time Lieutenant-Colonel Mix arrived with a force of cavalry and a section of the Third New York Artillery, under command of Lieutenant Day. This section opened fire with shot with good effect.

Near 10 o'clock the Ninth New Jersey Infantry was brought into action; also Morrison's battery, of the Third New York Artillery. By the aid of both of these forces the enemy was soon driven from his position. As soon as the battery ceased firing, the Ninth New Jersey forded the creek and charged upon the battery. The battery was taken, the old flag of the Union waved over it, and cheers were given and an interesting scene enacted.

While the bridge was being rebuilt, and while the "black pioneer brigade" was again making itself eminently useful, Colonel Heckmann pushed forward with the Ninth New Jersey, again engaging the enemy, capturing a Rodman gun, killing three of the enemy and taking a few more prisoners. Colonel Heckmann was soon after supported by Brigadier-General Wessell's brigade.

Just as the sun was sinking in the west we came upon two regiments of rebel infantry and two of their pieces of artillery, posted on a rise of ground behind a dense woods. The Ninth New Jersey once more advanced and drove the enemy back upon their guns after a rapid and sharp fire, when Captain Morrison's battery, of the Third New York Artillery, forced him to retire from his position, ceasing his fire altogether. Before the Ninth New Jersey got engaged, Captain Cole, with Company K., of the Third New York Cavalry, charged the enemy, clearing the road and driving the rebels to the woods. In this charge Franklin Chapman was wounded in the leg. Night having set in, we encamped about three miles and a half or four miles from Kinston. In the evening affair our losses were: —— Clifford, of the Ninth New Jersey, jaw broken; and —— Neucommer of the same regiment, taken prisoner.

DECEMBER 14, 1862.

Almost immediately after commencing anew our advance, we came upon a force of the enemy, entering into a heavy skirmish and then a general engagement.

The Ninth New Jersey advanced slowly down the road and then into the woods on either side. These skirmishers stood their ground until their entire stock of ammunition was exhausted, when the Eighty-fifth Pennsylvania was ordered up to support the Ninth. They did their duty well. This was at 10 o'clock. The enemy having brought his artillery into action, we returned a similar and much more effective fire from Captain Morrison's battery, of the Third New York Artillery, the latter being posted in a small field, on a rise of ground, within eight hundred yards of the enemy. Soon after Captains Schenck's and E. S. Jenney's batteries were brought into play, from different and the best available positions on either side of the road. The engagement having become more general, Brigadier-General Wessell's brigade was ordered up. It comprised the Eighty-fifth, One Hundred and First and One Hundred and Third Pennsylvania, and the Eighty-eighth, Ninety-second and Ninety-sixth New York. After the Forty-fifth, Seventeenth and Twenty-third Massachusetts Regiments had been ordered up, General Wessel, who was on the field, ordered the execution of a flank movement on the enemy's battery So it was that while a small portion of this force operated to the left, the remainder moved through a woods to the right, also flanking a swamp, and got a position on the line of an open field that enabled our men to play upon the enemy with intense effect and remarkable execution. The Ninth New Jersey, after sustaining a terriffic fire from the enemy, obtained a position close to the bridge, being handsomely supported by the Seventeenth Massachusetts, and then it was that we found ourselves almost on the banks of the Neuse river, with a long fortification on the opposite side. This fortification, one hundred and seventy-five feet long, thoroughly commanded all the approaches to the bridge. In it and supporting it were three companies of light artillery, four companies of heavy artillery, two North Carolina regiments, the Second, Seventeenth, Eighteenth and Twenty-third South Carolina Regiments, a portion of the Third North Carolina Cavalry, part of Major Nethercote's battalion, and the Raleigh detachment, under command of Colonel Molett, who was wounded in the leg—in all about six thousand strong.

The Forty-fifth and Twenty-third Massachusetts Regiments advanced to the right and helped to execute the flank movement. While the above was being done, Captain

Jacobs, with his company of the Third New York Cavalry and some light (Third New York) artillery, advanced on another road, to the right of the main column, and attracted as well as distracted the attention of the enemy.

Captain Jacobs came upon a regiment of rebel infantry, engaged them, drove them off with artillery, and then charged his men across, thereby saving quite an important bridge. Another diversion was created by Major Garrard, who was sent another road with a portion of his battalion of the Third New York Cavalry, one piece of Allis' Flying Artillery and two or three other light field pieces.

The gunboats, under command of Captain Murray, of the navy, and Lieutenant-Colonel Manchester, advanced up to the blockade and kept up a heavy firing. By this means General Evans was mystified regarding our order of movements that he would not bring the entire force under his command into operation in such a manner as to unitedly affect our main column.

After a sharp engagement for over three hours, we drove the enemy from his entrenchments and got possession of the bridge. The latter was fired in three places, but the Ninth New Jersey, a few of the Third New York Artillery, and the Provost-Marshall, Major Franklin, advanced in haste and put out the flames before the fires had done any material injury. Immediately our advance regiments crossed, when the Tenth Connecticut advanced upon the enemy and drove him over the fields forcing him to retreat to the further end of the town.

KINSTON, N. C., DEC. 14, 1862.
[AFTERNOON.]

Your correspondent crossed with the regiment, and Ninth New Jersey, and found lying on the bridge three or four men who had been shot down, smothered by the smoke, and burned by the flames; also an abundance of arms. Soon after we found that we had captured eleven pieces of artillery, taken 400 prisoners, (all of whom were paroled by the provost-marshal), 1,000 rounds of heavy ammunition, 500 stands of arms, a dozen or so gun carriages and a large quantity of commissary and quartermaster stores. These latter were solely saved through the exertions of Major Franklin, who found them in flames at the storehouses. We found the railroad depot in flames and that was also saved.

On looking around the town we found every evidence of our large and small shot having taken excellent effect. By the time two or three of our regiments had crossed, Major-General Foster dispatched Col. Potter, under a flag of truce, to communicate with Gen. Evans, and to demand a surrender of his forces. The flag was recognized. We found the rebel regiments retreating up the railroad and on the road and in various ways, straggling and otherwise, toward Goldsboro.

General Evans refused to comply, on high military grounds, etc. Soon after our artillery commenced anew to shell the rebels across the town, firing low—in fact so low that some of the shells swept very closely over our heads. General Evans then sent, by flag of truce, his compliments, etc., to Gen. Foster, and requested a place of safety for the women and children, as he intended to return the fire from his artillery. Our artillery ceased firing, and the women and children that could be found were conducted to a place of safety, when, we found, on preparing again for action, that the bird had flown ; that General Evans had succeeded during the flag of truce operations in safely conducting off what remained of his entire command. We then advanced a short distance and encamped for the night.

Our loss in wounded is between 100 and 120. Our total loss in killed, wounded and missing will not exceed 150. Colonel Gray, of the Ninety-sixth New York, was killed. Two or three other officers were wounded We cannot at this time ascertain the names of these.

All the combinations worked well, and General Foster deserves great credit for not only his plan of operations, but also the effective manner in which he carried them out.

General Foster will recommend Colonel Heckmann, of the Ninth New Jersey, for a brigadier-generalship. Colonel Hunt, of the Ninety-second New York, made two splendid charges with his regiment, and will also be recommended for a brigadier-generalship. The Tenth Connecticut lost heavily. They fought until they used up all their ammunition, and then advanced with the bayonet.

General Foster highly commends Colonel Ledlie, acting brigadier-general of artillery, for the energetic and skillful manner in which he operated a portion of his pieces, or those brought into action.

During the engagement, Captain Cole,

with Company K, of the Third New York Cavalry, was in position in the nearest open field, ready for a charge, if such a thing was possible, notwithstanding the shot and shell which fell around the company on all sides.

During the whole affair all the troops engaged behaved with great courage, and promptly executed the orders of the commanding generals.

We advance for Goldsboro at daylight to-morrow.

On the road, just after crossing the bridge, we found the following letter (it evidently had been dropped during the course of the enemy's hasty retreat):

GOLDSBORO, Dec. 14, 1862.

General Evans: All the men I have here have been sent to you. You received them last night. Rogers is nearly with you, 400 strong. I understand from rumors that three other regiments are on their way here from Petersburg.

J. A. J. BRADFORD.

We learn that the Rogers force arrived just in time to retreat.

The rebels destroyed some eighty or ninety bales of cotton. This we found burning as we entered the town. Most of it belonged to a Scotchman named Nicolo.

During the evening a house accidentally got on fire, when the flames communicated to three or four others, all being destroyed. Energetic measures were taken to subdue the flames.

The provost guard arrangement works admirably. Little or no damage is being done. The good conduct of the troops is remarkable.

FIFTH DAY.

IN THE FIELD, DEC. 15, 1862.

We moved out of Kinston at a very early hour this morning, and marched up the line of the Neuse River on the side opposite to that place. The road lay through a section of country hilly and comparatively poor. During the day we came upon the enemy's pickets and drove them in, taking three or four prisoners. By sunset we had marched seventeen miles. We then bivouacked for the night. This day's march was considered a very good one, considering the fatigued condition of the troops. On marching out of Kinston and recrossing the river the bridge we so fortunately saved the day previous was totally destroyed, in order to defeat any design on the part of General Evans to follow up and attack us in the rear. When the main column halted for the night Major Garrard, with his battalion of the Third New York Cavalry, and a section of Captain Jenney's battery of the Third New York Artillery, were sent forward to dash into and take a small town on the Neuse, known as Whitehall. To do this we had to go a distance of three and a half miles from the main column. This we accomplished at a full gallop; but, notwithstanding we pushed forward so rapidly, we found on our arrival the bridge over the river in flames. We also learned that a Virginia regiment had just retreated across the bridge, and that they would be heavily reinforced on the following morning. The Major immediately ordered a reconnoissance of the whole position by dismounted cavalrymen. In this reconnoissance we found previous reports confirmed, in that we discovered a rebel gunboat on the other side of the river.

To destroy the gunboat which was not fully completed, was one of our principal objects; but to do it in the face of an enemy, concealed in the woods on the opposite bank, was a different matter. In order to cast a heavy reflection of light on the enemy, we set fire to large quantities of turpentine, in barrels, in sheds and otherwise. This rendered the scene one of peculiar and lively interest. The flames ascended in all forms and to various heights, communicating to and firing many of the adjacent trees. During all this time the enemy laid low in the woods, only firing one or two small arms.

After brief deliberation, the Major determined to call upon some one to volunteer and swim the river; then, after swimming it, to board the gunboat and fire it. To do this daring deed, Henry Butler, of Company C, Third New York Cavalry, volunteered. Our artillery was ordered up, and opened with shell to the right and left of the bridge. Butler then undressed, ran down the bank, plunged into the river, and swam to the opposite side. He then started to get a fire brand at the burning bridge, when the enemy opened fire on him. Butler instantly turned and ran for the river, followed by a couple of the enemy (who quickly sprang from their hiding places), jumped into the water, was again fired upon, and finally reached his old position without injury. For this gallant act the Major highly complimented Butler on the spot and while Butler was in a situation not observable in civilized, unwarlike society. We then gave the enemy a severe dose of canister, and, finding that we could not well get over to the gunboat, we battered it to pieces with shot and shell. The vessel was a small one, flat bottomed, intended for fast river navigation, designed for one or two guns, built somewhat after the form of the Merrimac, iron plating and all. We then returned to camp, having acccomplished our purpose.

In connection with our movements to-day I may add that the enemy was completely outwitted. From the fact of our having fought hard to save Kinston bridge, and then crossed to the opposite side, occupying the town, the enemy prepared to meet us at Mosely Hall—a small town adjacent to the line of the Goldsboro and Kinston railroad—supposing that we intended proceeding to that town along the right bank of the Neuse. Instead of that, as will be observed by what is above, we passed up on the other side, leaving Mosely Hall, with its armed force, far to the right.

SIXTH DAY.

WHITEHALL, Dec. 16, P. M.

The column again moved at an early hour this morning in the direction of Whitehall. As we neared the town an open space revealed our approach to the enemy, the latter being concealed in a thick woods on the opposite side of the river. Heavy skirmishing immediately ensued between the Ninth New Jersey and three regiments of rebels. Major Garrard who was in advance of the column, with three pieces of artillery and a squadron of cavalry, passed over a high hill behind the skirmishers, in full sight of the enemy, until he got to the left of those in action, and then opened with his artillery. In a few minutes other artillery came up, when the Major ceased firing. Although his cavalry force was in a position of great exposure, under a heavy fire for quite a while, still the loss was quite trifling.

Under cover of action on both sides, Major Garrard, with his command, pressed on past

Whitehall, and made a rapid march (a distance of over twenty miles) to Mount Olive Station, a small place situated on the line of the Wilmington and Goldsboro railroad. While Major Garrard was away, in order to cover his operations, General Foster entered into a regular engagement at Whitehall.

The enemy, having destroyed the bridge over the river, showed that he labored under the impression that we would attempt to cross at this point; whereas, if he had not been so fast, he would have discovered that it was our intention to burn the bridge on the previous evening. The engagement at Whitehall lasted for over three hours. The enemy operated against us with a force of about five or six thousand infantry and three batteries of artillery. The Ninth New Jersey Volunteers, General Wessell's brigade, and a couple of Massachusetts regiments, were engaged in the fight. A few other regiments were brought under fire ; and, as they lost a few men, I suppose they claim to being in the fight also. My accounts of the killed and wounded will explain the engagements in which the regiments participated. Neither in the battles of Kinston or Whitehall was over half our forces engaged at one time, especially not in the latter.

The better to deceive the enemy, General Foster made feint of rebuilding the bridge under fire. A feint was also made to cross the river; and a few of one of our Massachusetts regiments, not knowing that they were only to make a feint, actually swam across the river and got on the opposite bank. Of course they were forced back. Under the direction of Colonel Ledlie (acting brigadier-general), our artillery was so admirably posted and gallantly worked that we silenced the enemy's fire, and drove him, infantry, artillery and all, away far back from the river bank. After this we could, of course, have crossed the river; but the scope of General Foster's plan tended still more to deceive the enemy. Under cover of infantry firing and the working of two sections of artillery we passed on without further molestations and went into camp for the night several miles the other side of Whitehall.

MOUNT OLIVE STATION, Dec. 16, 1862.

On leaving the main column we pressed rapidly on, on regular and by-roads until we reached a swamp. Here we struck a turpentine path, and after a full gallop of a distance of over four miles, came out at this station at 3 p. m. This action was a perfect surprise to the people of the place. The ticket agent was selling tickets; passengers were loitering around waiting for the cars, the mail for Wilmington laid ready on the platform, and a few paroled prisoners were in readiness to go to Wilmington, probably to fight again. As a matter of course, for the time being, Major Garrard put everybody under arrest. The telegraph wire was immediately and afterwards effectually cut and destroyed by Captain Willson, of the Third New York Cavalry. Mount Olive is seventeen miles from Goldsboro, and as I have specified before, immediately on the line of the Goldsboro and Wilmington railroad.

Captains Willson and Pond, with their respective commands of the Third New York Cavalry, were sent seven miles in the direction of Wilmington, to destroy an extensive bridge and trestle work. This they accomplished with great labor, after a few minutes' skirmishing and joined our main forces by dusk. In connection with the destruction of these bridges they also destroyed the track and set fire to cross ties in several places. While this was being done, Captain Jacobs, with a company of the Third New York Cavalry, and one piece of Allis' Flying artillery, was sent three and a half miles in the direction of Goldsboro, on the line of the railroad, to destroy the tracks, some culverts and a bridge. Just as Captain

Jacobs reached the three and a half mile point the mail train from Goldsboro came rattling down. The engineer on the train, in coming around a sharp turn, observed ahead a heavy dark smoke, immediately whistled down brakes, and reversed his order of proceeding. Notwithstanding this, Captain Jacobs was enabled to bring his pieces of artillery into such a position as to give the retreating train the force of three shells. After doing his business, and well and ably developing the bumps of destruction in North Carolina, he joined us at Mount Olive just about sundown.

By this time we at Mount Olive Station had taken up a large extent of the track, destroyed the switches and did all the damage we could; then, about 8 o'clock, we set out for a change of base, made several strategical movements through woods and swamps and reached the camp of the great army about midnight, having cut across, as explained above, without moving on any main road more than five minutes at a time.

On leaving Mount Olive I paused for a moment to behold the sight presented to our view. I saw the railroad apparently on fire for miles in extent, huge fires of ties and warping rails, and the blank amazement that was but too evident on the faces of our newly released prisoners. The woods were bright and radient with the reflected light; our hidden road was also illuminated, and all nature seemed changed—as the light reflected on the water in the swamp—if not to one of beauty, at least to a great degree of attractiveness. As we left, the boys gave three cheers for the Major's success, and the same was highly complimented by General Foster, on making his report to that officer.

We had hardly left Mount Olive Station over an hour when the enemy came down as near as he could with a so-called "Merrimac Railroad Car," and shelled the woods for quite a while.

SEVENTH DAY.

ON THE FIELD, Dec 17, 1862.

We resumed our line of march this morning and got on a high hill and in full sight of a large force of the enemy drawn up in line on the railroad, without meeting anything of importance to impede our progress.

Having the advantage of position, being on a hill, over a mile from the railroad, with an entirely open country before us, the river on our right and a dense wood to the left—we opened on the enemy with shell. For a very short space of time the rebels stood their ground; but so accurately did we get the range of their position, rapidly throwing in the shells, that the enemy broke front and line, and commenced a precipitate retreat across the river on the railroad bridge. We kept up our firing with considerable rapidity, and by that means cut off the retreat of two rebel regiments, who fell back into thick woods on the other side of the railroad Colonel Ledlie then moved a battery to within less than half a mile of the enemy's position. The Ninth New Jersey was sent, to support the battery, across an open field and afterwards beyond it, until the regiment got close to the right of the railroad bridge, and a short distance from the enemy and the river. While these operations were being carried out, the Seventeenth Massachusetts, under command of Lieutenant-Colonel Fellows, moved to the left, into the woods, waded through a mill stream, and came out on the railroad line directly in front of the enemy. By this time and while the Seventeenth was slowly advancing, the enemy commenced a rapid fire of shot and shell from a battery concealed in the woods across the river, and to the left of the bridge, looking from our position, as also from their iron-clad railroad car, occupying a position on the other side of the river, close to the entrance to the bridge At this point they also had sharpshooters, who tried hard, but did not well succeed in picking off our men.

By the time the action had become tolerably heavy we heard the whistle of an approaching train, and soon after learned from prisoners that the rebel General Pettigrew had just arrived with reinforcements in the way of a big brigade.

One of our shells was seen to pass along a platform car, thereby creating so much confusion as to delay General Pettigrew from coming immediately into action. Having got range of the train, we threw the shells in so fast that in a little while it moved further off and out of range of our guns.

The object of General Foster's penetrating so far inland being to destroy this railroad bridge, he now gave orders to have it burned. Colonel Heckmann, who got the order, called for volunteers to carry into effect the general's desire. Many volunteered from the Seventeenth Massachusetts and Ninth New-Jersey Regiments, so the Colonel selected some from each regiment to go and do the work. Several advances were made to fire, but our men were driven back. In one of the advances a former adjutant of the Seventeenth was dangerously wounded.

Finally, Lieutenant Graham, of the Rocket Battery, and now acting aid to Colonel Heckmann, and Wm. Lemons, a private in the Ninth New Jersey, advanced under the enemy's heavy firing, when Lieutenant Graham got near enough to, and did fire, the bridge.

As soon as we saw the bridge in flames the General gave orders to have the railroad track destroyed. Two Massachusetts regiments, who had been lying in reserve, stacked arms and rushed upon the track with yells and cheers, and did the work of destruction at short notice. The rails and ties were thoroughly destroyed by physical power and the effect of fire.

General Foster having successfully accomplished all his plans, and more, to day determined to withdraw his forces from the field, and to fall back to the first convenient camping place for the night. The column was got in motion (each regiment cheering the General as it passed), and we had advanced a considerable distance (probably two miles), with the supply train, etc. in front. When the rebels, seeing the last brigade, Col. Lee's, about to move, and some distance from the artillery, took courage and rushed out of the woods on the other side of the railroad, and gave the rallying cry and yell that follows it. Immediately afterwards two South Carolina regiments, who had come from Franklin, fired a volley and then charged with the bayonet on Morrison's battery. The enemy were allowed to get rather close to the battery, when the guns opened on them with canister. Belger's battery put in a powerful cross fire, and Col. Lee's brigade wheeled into line and did excellent execution. The rebels made this bayonet charge with great dash and courage, but, notwithstanding, they were repulsed with great loss of life, and an amusing and astonishing precipitancy.

Of course, this latter movement on the part of the rebels had the effect of halting our column for several hours. Not knowing but that they might be in strong force this side of the river, we made every preparation to enter into a regular engagement. However after a renewed fight, lasting nearly two hours, we again silenced the enemy's fire, and pursued our retrograde movement. In the last fight the rebels opened from two batteries instead of one—their iron plated car—and brought into action their infantry on both sides of the river.

In the battle of this bridge the rebels had, as prisoners report, between eight and ten thousand troops engaged. We never had over one-third of our force engaged. About nine o'clock p. m. our army bivouacked for the night, between Whitehall and the Goldsboro railroad bridge.

While the battle was progressing at the bridge, Major Fitzsimmons with his battalions of the Third New York Cavalry made a dash against Dudley Station, on the line of the Wilmington railroad, five miles from the Goldsboro railroad bridge, took prisoners several rebel pickets, captured and destroyed a train of four cars, took up three miles of the railroad track, burned some trestle work, a bridge, and other little *et ceteras*, including a most complete destruction of the telegraph line, and joined the main column without loss to his command. The Major also repeated a similar experiment at Everett Station, on the line of the same railroad. Major Garrard with his battalion of the Third New York Cavalry went (while the main army was moving) early in the morning to Tompkins bridge, over the Neuse river. He took with him a section of Ransom's Twenty-third New York Artillery. On arriving in the vicinity of the bridge Captain Jacobs, with his company of cavalry, was ordered to charge down to it. He did so, found the bridge in flames, and received fire from the enemy. It will again be seen that the enemy was deceived in regard to a crossing of the Neuse. The Major immediately opened with his artillery, and at the same time despatched a messenger to inform General Foster with regards to his position, condition, etc. As soon as General Foster received the information he reinforced the Major with four pieces of artillery from Angell's battery and the Forty-third Massachusetts Regiment under command of Colonel Holbrook. After a fight of over two hours we silenced the enemy's heavy guns and musketry, and returned to the main column with a loss of one killed and four wounded. Before leaving, our forces could go anywhere in that neighborhood, along the banks of the river, without being fired at. The rebels had eight pieces of artillery and four regiments of infantry at this bridge. About 10 o'clock Allis' Flying artillery, and

Companies G, A, and D, of the Third New York Cavalry, in attempting to join the main column from another direction, were attacked by two pieces of the rebel's artillery, and, as is supposed, about a regiment of rebel infantry. In less than fifteen minutes our artillery silenced that of the enemy.

During the engagement a chaplain of one of the Massachusetts regiments, who was on the field, seeing one of the men of Battery B, Third New York Artillery, being borne off wounded, said to him: "Were you supported by Divine inspiration?" "No!" was the reply, "we were supported by the Ninth New Jersey."

On the battle field at Whitehall, Colonel Ledlie (chief of artillery) received a very slight wound on the hand from one of the rebels' shells.

During the progress of our operations there were brought into action, at various times, Belger's battery, batteries A, B, C, D, E, H, I, F, and K, of the Third New York

Artillery, and the Twenty-third and Twenty-fourth (independent) New York Batteries. The whole of our artillery was worked admirably.

Captain Morrison's battery of the Third New York Artillery had three men wounded, and lost the same number of horses. Captain Morrison took at the battle of Kinston forty-one prisoners, including two commissioned officers. At the battle of the railroad bridge he took seven more prisoners. When his battery was charged by the South Carolina regiments he kept up a steady fire until every round of his ammunition was gone, and then gave way to Captain Belger. Captain Riggs' battery was also engaged in helping to repulse the charge of the South Carolina brigade. In the battles of the 16th and 17th Captain Ammon's battery did good execution, and without sustaining any casualties in the company. These three batteries while in action, were under the immediate command of Major Kennedy. At Mount Olive

Station, among the private papers of the postmaster was found the following:

"Whereas, we, the people of the counties of Wayne and Dublin, have seen a proclamation from the black republican president, Abraham Lincoln, calling for seventy-five thousand men, (and a call made on North Carolina among the rest), for the purpose of subjugating our Southern brethren of the Confederate States, who are asking nothing but for their rights to be respected and their institutions let alone, the interest of North Carolina being identified with the said Confederate States, we, as her citizens, deem it highly necessary to express our views to the world, irrespective of former party ties; therefore

Resolved, That the example of our patriotic forefathers is too plainly set before us to be unmindful of our duty. We know the cause of the Confederate States to be the supreme interest of North Carolina; therefore, we pledge our fortunes, our lives and our most sacred honors in the maintenance of the said cause.

Resolved, That, for the aid and furtherance of said cause and the defence of our homes and our rights, we will form a military company for the purpose of drilling that we may be the better prepared to defend our homes and our country.

Resolved, That we call upon all good citizens to sustain us and give us their aid for the support of our company.

Resolved, That the manly and patriotic courage of His Excellency, John W. Ellis, in ordering our forts taken and held by troops of this State, and his independent denial of troops to Abe Lincoln to sustain him in his diabolical policy, meets the entire approbation of this company and this community."

Our total loss is between four and five hundred. In all we took over five hundred prisoners.

EIGHTH DAY.

DECEMBER 18, 1862.

The army marched this day to within seven miles of Kinston. We had to pass through woods on fire; some of the natives had purposely and some of our men having accidentally (the latter through the medium of their camp fires) communicated flames to the turpentine trees. Though the scene was novel and pleasing still it was dangerous, and at times somewhat more than this.

NINTH DAY.

DECEMBER, 19, 1862.

Your correspondent left the army about seven o'clock this morning, and, after a horseback ride of over forty miles, reached New Berne by sundown. When he left, the army was on its way to New Berne.

THE LATEST.

NEW BERNE, Dec. 20, 1862.

During the progress of the late expedition we came upon large quantities of cotton and turpentine. Our advance was so peculiar and rapid that the rebels did not have time to burn it, although we occasionally found large quantities on fire.

Our entire movement was greatly facilitated by Captain Sleight, to whose energetic course of action was due the keeping of our supply, etc., trains. General Foster highly complimented Captain Sleight for the ability with which he conducted his department.

I forgot to mention in my account of the engagement at Goldsboro railroad bridge that the enemy, on finding that our troops were outflanking them by wading through a mill stream, hoisted the gate at the mill and let the water rush down with astonishing impetuosity. By this means one or two of our men were drowned, while others still pushed on, with the water up to their armpits, regardless of the difficulty.

We learn by flag of truce, from the rebels at Kinston, that their (the rebels) loss is between eight and nine hundred, and that the two South Carolina regiments that charged Morrison's battery, lost in that charge about three hundred and fifty men; their color bearer was shot three times.

BRILLIANT CONDUCT OF THE UNION TROOPS.

Kinston, N. C., Dec. 15. 1862.

An important movement has long been on foot looking towards the capture of Goldsboro and Weldon, and the severance of one rebel railroad line of communication connecting the cotton states with the capital of the so-called confederacy; Preparations have for some time been carried to enable the force which was to engage in the attempt to push it to a successful issue. The time has now come when the object and the means of execution of this movement may be safely revealed. The object of the expedition was to capture Kinston, and then to take Goldsboro, thereby cutting the Wilmington and Weldon railroad, which would isolate Wilmington and effectually cut off its supplies and reinforcements. That, I believe, was the object of the expedition. The first portion of the work has been accomplished—the capture of Kinston; and the other portion is in a fair way of being carried successfully out to the letter.

The forces under General Foster left New Berne on Thursday, the 11th, and moved up the Trent road, along the Trent River, about ten miles, when the division halted for the night. On Friday the march was resumed at sunrise, the Ninth New Jersey having the extreme advance, followed by Wessell's brigade, one of General Peck's brigade, recently sent from Suffolk, with Company B, Third New York Artillery, Captain Morrison. Then followed the brigade of Acting Brigadier-General Amory consisting of four Massachusetts regiments.

Acting Brigadier-General Lee's brigade of Massachusetts regiments came next, Colonel Stevenson's brigade, also of Massachusetts regiments, brought up the rear with four regiments. Acting Brigadier-General Ledlie, of the Third New York Artillery, had command of the artillery, consisting of the Third New York Artillery and Belger's battery, First Rhode Island Artillery. Colonel Mix's Third New York Cavalry, Lieutenant-Colonel Mix in command, were employed as scouts on the advance and on the sides of the line of march, and as provost-guards to protect houses along the road.

On Friday night the column halted within eleven miles of Kinston, and encamped in line of battle, no fires being allowed and all unusual noises prohibited. The troops did not get into camp until 9 o'clock. Skirmishing continued all day between cavalry of the rebels and Mix's cavalry, in which we lost two men prisoners and one wounded. We captured fifteen or sixteen of the rebel cavalry, and killed and wounded several.

On Saturday morning at 7 o'clock the line of march was resumed towards Kinston at a slow pace, as the enemy were beginning to appear in some force in front, to a point where the Whitehall, and main Kinston roads unite, about seven miles from Kinston. This point was reached at about 11 o'clock on Saturday morning, and then it was that it was expected that the rebels would offer battle, as it was a strong position. Our troops were formed in line of battle in an open field on the left of the road which ran to Whitehall, in front of a wood, which it was supposed covered the enemy's main force. A small creek ran across the road 500 yards to the right and in front of our line of battle, over which was a bridge, which the rebels had destroyed, and out of the debris of which they had erected a breastwork and planted two six-pounders, rifled, sweeping the road. Morrison's battery was put forward to the right of the road, and taking a position on a small hill 250 yards from the rebel battery, opened fire. The enemy hotly replied with grape and canister, sweeping the road, but doing no damage. Morrison continued to shell the battery and the woods on either side for nearly an hour, when the enemy began to retire. Just as the enemy were about retiring, the Ninth

New Jersey were deployed as skirmishers to the left of the road, and advancing under fire, they crossed the creek on a mill dam, flanked the rebel battery, and, taking it by storm, captured a rifled six-pounder and several prisoners. The rebels retreated hastily and succeeded in saving the other six-pounder, but left six killed and wounded. Three hours were consumed in the reconstruction of the bridge. When completed the infantry and, artillery crossed and marched towards Kinston, about three and a half miles, and halted for the night, in line of battle, with strong pickets out. The enemy made but feeble resistance to the advance of our forces, Mix's cavalry driving them like chaff before them. The night passed quietly, a little affair between pickets, without result, breaking the monotony of the night.

On Sunday morning, at daybreak, Mix's cavalry and Wessell's brigade began to advance, feeling their way cautiously up the road about two miles, when the enemy's pickets were met and driven back through a piece of woods about three-quarters of a mile, when they retired upon the main body of the enemy, six thousand strong, under command of Brigadier-General Evans, of Ball's Bluff notoriety. His forces consisted of three regiments of South Carolina infantry, the balance, of artillery, cavalry and infantry, was made up of North Carolina troops. Here our advance halted and the artillery was ordered to the front, and at 10.30 the artillery opened on the enemy. The rebels were found to be drawn up in line of battle, on a ground partially wooded and covered with a dense underbrush, with their artillery in the center and on either flank. They formed their line nearly in the shape of a triangle, with the base towards our forces. Our line was formed with the Ninth New Jersey on the right, Wessell's brigade in the center and left; Behind, in a second line, was the Twenty-third Massachusetts Regiment, on the right the Forty-fourth and Forty-fifth and other regiments of Amory's brigade, Stevenson's and Lee's brigades being held in reserve. Our artillery was placed in position on the right, centre and left of the line. The battle was begun by the artillery at 10.30, and continued uninterruptedly until about 1.30 o'clock, when the enemy commenced to retreat. But a short time elapsed after the artillery duel had begun before the infantry got to work in earnest, and the musketry became very rapid and hot. The fight was quite lively until 1 o'clock, but not at very close quarters, when the rebels began to fall back, and the Ninth New Jersey were thrown out as skirmishers, and Wessell's brigade pushed forward in pursuit. Our batteries were then thrown around to the right of the road, and fired upon the retreating rebels, but with little effect. The enemy fell back hastily nearly a mile, and crossed the bridge leading into Kinston, the Ninth New Jersey following closely in pursuit. As the last rebel regiment crossed the bridge the rebels applied the match to it, and as it had been prepared for the purpose, the fire gained some headway; but the Ninth New Jersey came up in time to extinguish the fire soon before it had done much damage.

After crossing the bridge one rebel brigade retreated in the direction of Goldsboro and the other in the direction of Snow Hill, on the road to Weldon. General Evans, with his South Carolina troops, retreated towards Goldsboro, our artillery throwing shells on the retreating columns.

Our division immediately crossed the bridge and occupied Kinston, the rebels on their retreat burning a quantity of cotton, a locomotive and some cars. Our troops held the town until yesterday morning, when they left the town and moved forward in a northerly direction, after burning the bridge over the Neuse River. We captured on the battle field four hundred prisoners, eleven pieces of artillery on this side of the bridge and three on the other, making fourteen guns in all, taken from them. A large number of small arms, perhaps eight hundred, were taken. Our loss was one hundred and sixty, killed and wounded. That of the enemy about one hundred and twenty-five, as they were more protected. The only officers killed on our side were Colonel Gray, of the Ninety-sixth New York Volunteers; Captain Wells and Lieutenant Perkins, of the Tenth Connecticut; we captured a lieutenant-colonel of a South Carolina regiment, and several other officers. The Twenty-third Massachusetts, Major Chambers commanding, captured seventy officers and men of the Twenty-third South Carolina Regiment. The mudsills are a little ahead of the chivalry this time.

Our forces are now on the march, and I halt behind to send off this report. You will hear from me again by the first conveyance. Our troops are in excellent spirits and eager to push forward and reap the fruits of our victory. You may rest assured that General Foster will follow up his advantage to a successful issue. I forgot to mention that Company K, Mix's Third New York Cavalry, charged and captured three pieces of artillery, with caissons, horses and all, in the most gallant manner.

SCENE OF THE DEATH OF COLONEL GRAY.

NEW BERNE, N. C., Dec. 16, 1862.

Colonel Boler of the Forty-sixth Massachusetts, has returned from General Foster's expedition, and reports the successful capture of the town of Kinston by the Union troops, and their advance towards Goldsboro, the junction of the Atlantic and North Carolina and the Wilmington and Weldon railroads.

There was some fighting for three days— Friday, Saturday, and Sunday, last—the enemy disputing our advance with pertinacity wherever the ground favored them. They are reported to have had a force of 15,000 under command of General Evans, of Ball's Bluff fame. Their loss is heavy in killed, wounded and prisoners, five hundred of the latter having fallen into our hands. Our loss is one hundred and fifty to two hundred and fifty in killed, wounded and missing.

The principal fight was a few miles beyond Kinston, where the enemy had intrenched themselves. The Third New York Cavalry, Colonel Mix's, had a hand to hand conflict with the Second North Carolina Cavalry. The New Yorkers routed the North Carolinians after a hard fight. All the Union troops are reported to have behaved well, exhibiting in many instances great courage and fearlessness.

Our wounded were placed in unoccupied houses in Kinston and the dead buried.

The advance continues toward Goldsboro; but before reaching that point we shall have to encounter further and still stronger opposition. With the large and well disciplined forces of Generals Foster and Wessell, every obstruction will be overcome, and the object sought attained.

Twelve miles beyond Kinston, at a place called Mosely Hall, the enemy have a battery of ten heavy guns, so planted as to deal a very destructive fire upon an advancing foe.

In the attack upon Lieutenant-Colonel Manchester's transports in the Neuse River the rebels suffered severely as reported by a deserter this morning. The shells from the Allison fell directly in the midst of the battery, killing and wounding several, and, for a time, dispersing the working force of the battery, together with an infantry reserve of some two hundred men, with two regiments at hand.

The Ocean Wave was fired upon from an open field by a force of one hundred and ten North Carolina rebel troops, commanded by Captain Whitfield.

The first brush with the enemy commenced about 8 o'clock on Friday morning, about twenty miles from New Berne, on the main road to Kinston, a little to the right of Winton when Company B, Captain Marshall, Third New York Artillery, encountered them.

The enemy's force consisted of one company of cavalry and four companies of infantry, of Major Nethercote's North Carolina battalion. After a brief skirmish we dispersed the rebels, killing two, wounded and missing amounting to fifty. Our loss was two wounded and four missing.' The advance then moved on, after crossing a bridge, partly destroyed, over a creek, and being delayed an hour in fixing the same. Captain N. encamped the same night within nine miles of Kinston.

On Saturday morning Company K, Captain Cole, Third New York Cavalry, took the advance, and while moving forward captured two prisoners, belonging to Nethercote's battalion, who gave some valuable information, proceeded thence to South-

west creek, about five miles from Kinston.
On Captain Cole's approach, the enemy
were found engaged in endeavoring to destroy the bridge over the creek. Captain
Cole dismounted a platoon, who fired a volley
upon the enemy while they were at work.
The enemy then retreated, but soon after
fired from a battery of two six-pounders,
howitzers, upon our advance, wounding one
man—a private, named John Costello—who
was shot through the head.

Colonel Heckmann, of the Ninth. New
Jersey (the advance guard of the infantry),
here came forward and ordered the Ninth to
deploy as skirmishers. This order was
quickly executed, and had the effect of
partly dispersing the enemy; and Schenck's
Third New York battery coming up, fired
about a dozen shells, driving the enemy
entirely away. On the Ninth New Jersey
crossing the bridge, four of the enemy were
found dead, the wounded being carried on
with the retreating enemy. The Ninth suc-

ceeded in capturing one of their howitzers, which was brought into New Berne this morning.

As soon as Captain Cole had crossed the bridge, following the New Jersey Ninth, he was ordered forward by Colonel Heckmann, and his company directed to act as scouts to find the position of the enemy. They had proceeded about eighty or one hundred rods beyond the pickets of the Ninth when the advance guard of Company K was fired upon by a concealed body of the enemy, and Private Chapman wounded in the thigh. Captain Cole then halted, and Colonel Heckmann ordered a part of the Ninth New Jersey forward to skirmish through the woods. The enemy were found in the edge of the woods when a lively fire commenced between our skirmishers and the foe. The entire Ninth was then ordered forward, and the rebels commenced firing sharply from a battery of three howitzers, with grape and canister. A section of two pieces of Schenck's battery was now ordered up, and returned the enemy's grape and canister with twelve-pound shells. The gallant Jerseymen kept advancing steadily upon the enemy, committing great havoc in their ranks by their unerring aim, until finally the rebels were driven from the woods, and obliged to fall back about half a mile to an open field, skirted by woods. The fight ended about dark, when our advance guard encamped upon the scene of battle. It is a singular fact, notwithstanding the conspicuous part taken and gallantry displayed in this skirmish by the Ninth New Jersey in their advancing movements, but one man was wounded in the whole regiment. But they suffered subsequently. The number of the enemy killed and wounded is unknown, but supposed to be heavy.

The advance laid upon the field all night without molestation. On the following morning (Sunday), about 7.30, the first gun was fired upon the enemy by one of Captain Cole's pickets, and the report spread that the rebels were approaching in force. Colonel Heckmann had the brigade of which he is acting-commander immediately drawn up in line of battle, with the intrepid Ninth still in the advance. After waiting about half an hour, and finding the enemy did not approach, the Ninth was ordered forward, with skirmishers to the right and left, the main body being in the Kinston road. They were then within about three miles from Kinston, and while moving were occasionally saluted with a shot from the enemy's skirmishers. In a short time the firing became more general, and as the Jerseymen went on, closely followed by the brave boys of Company K of the Third New York Cavalry, they returned the fire briskly. After reaching a point bordering on a piece of woods, the rebels commenced firing artillery, nearly raking the road on which our troops were advancing. They then fired to the right and left, to prevent a flank movement, which was attempted by Colonel Heckmann. The fight began now in earnest, and as our infantry and artillery were ordered up, regiment by regiment. General Wessell rode forward, immediately followed by General Foster; and while the fighting in front was going on, the manœuvering of our forces so as to outflank the enemy was begun. General Foster ordered Colonel Heckmann to take his brigade to the right, by the river road, and attack the enemy on their left flank;. the artillery, consisting of the Third New York Artillery, Belger's Rhode Island battery, Schenck's battery, and two or three others, closely following the infantry. After getting into position a terrible fire was opened upon the enemy from the front and flank. This was withstood with great fortitude and bravery by the enemy for about four hours, when a dashing charge, made by several of our regiments, caused the rebels to break and retreat in confusion across the bridge, over the Neuse, clear to and through the village of Kinston and beyond. Some places they crossed in their flight up the river, to the left, the water was so deep that it reached the bellies of our cavalry horses while in pursuit. The Neuse River bridge had been saturated with turpentine in places, and as the enemy retired in their great haste they imperfectly set fire to it; but the fire was easily extinguished by the aid of the artillery buckets, used for watering the horses. It was here we met our saddest loss, almost, as it were, by accident. Colonel Gray of the Ninty-sixth New York was at work with his regiment, endeavoring to put out the fire, when a loaded musket, thrown away by a flying rebel, caught fire and exploded, the charge entering the body of the Colonel, and inflicting a wound which caused instant death. His body was brought to New Berne by Company K, and will be sent to New York.

The bridge was soon in condition to permit

the infantry to cross with perfect safety, our artillery having in the meantime opened from the bridge upon the enemy, who had been rallied and was again formed in line of battle about a mile beyond the village of Kinston. The enemy made no reply but with artillery, but fell back behind a high hill out of sight. About 2 p. m. General Foster ordered troops to enter the town, when it was occupied, and three brigades sent about two miles beyond. Seven or eight houses were burned in Kinston, some say by accident and some by design, after our men got in. The rebels burned a great amount of corn and cotton before leaving the place. The Ninth New Jersey, taking the advance again, forced the rebels from behind the hill where they had made a stand, to a point about three miles from Kinston, when the troops encamped for the night (Sunday).

After reaching the town, Captain Cole of Company K, Third New York Cavalry, was ordered to proceed down the river to the blockade, and where a battery had been erected to play upon our gunboats if they attempted to ascend the river. Captain Cole, on arriving at the place—a sort of half circular fort, with breastworks a mile and a half long—ascertained from a negro that the rebels had moved six brass pieces about six hours before he reached there; that they had more guns there, and that a guard had been left to protect them until they could be secured, the rebels not having enough horses to get them all away. Captain Cole attempted to surround the fort and capture what there was remaining in it, when the guard discovered his force and decamped for the woods without firing a shot. Company K charged on the fort and took possession thereof, capturing everything in it. The armament remaining was found to consist of seven guns, including one eight-inch columbiad, two thirty-two-pounder iron guns, and four six-pounder iron guns. The four latter were found to be loaded, primed and ready to be fired; but the brisk movements of Captain Cole and his daring company prevented the execution of the latter deadly operation. Company K and its commander have been highly complimented by the commanding General for their gallantry on this occasion. A small amount of provisions, clothing, etc., was found in the fort, which was left. The four six-pounders were brought away; the columbiad and the thirty-twos, being too heavy to be removed, were spiked and the carriages burned. Captain Cole reached Kinston about midnight with the trophies. The next morning about 5 o'clock he received orders from General Foster to return to New Berne with seven pieces—two brass and five iron—captured with other trophies. The two brass pieces were the same captured from us at Little Washington about three months ago. Captain Cole also brings the remains of Colonel Gray, of the Ninety-sixth New York, killed on Neuse bridge. On his way down Captain Cole captured eight rebels and brought them into New Berne. Three belonged to South Carolina and four to Georgia.

The New Jersey Ninth captured the regimental flag of a South Carolina regiment before crossing the Neuse bridge, and carry it as a trophy of their gallantry.

Most of the 500 rebels captured and paroled by General Foster belonged to South Carolina and Georgia.

The conduct of the Tenth Connecticut Regiment is spoken of in the highest terms. They, with the New Jersey Ninth, were particularly distinguished for their bravery, and suffered the most.

THE GUNBOATS IN THE BATTLE.

[Our New Berne Correspondence.]

NEW BERNE, N. C., Dec. 16, 1862.

An expedition, consisting of the gunboats Delaware, Seymour and Shawsheen, of the navy, under the command of Commander Murray, United States Navy, and the steamboats Ocean Wave, Allison, North State, Port Royal, and Wilson, manned by the Marine Artillery and commanded by Colonel Manchester, left this point on Thursday last, the 11th inst., to proceed up the Neuse River to co-operate with the land forces under General Foster in his advance toward Kinston, or more properly to effect a diversion in General Foster's favor. Owing to lack of water the gunboats were unable to go up the river more than fifteen or eighteen miles, and were compelled to stop and allow the affair to be carried on by the Marine Artillery flotilla alone. Colonel Manchester assumed command of the expedition from that point, and resolutely pushed up toward Kinston, determined to reach the village and participate in its capture. The low state of the water alone prevented Commander Murray from carrying his heavy gunboats to the town.

Colonel Manchester met but little resistance going up, a few scattering shots being fired at him by guerillas on the banks. He experienced much difficulty, however, in getting ahead rapidly, because of the bars and shoals, upon which the boats grounded. But all obstacles being overcome, they reached a point within two miles of Kinston on Saturday afternoon, when they suddenly found themselves under the fire of an eleven gun battery, which opened on the Allison, the leading boat, as she rounded a point of land and appeared full in view of the enemy's formidable work, and not over 1,200 yards distant. The river was here only about one hundred feet in width, with shoals on either side of the channel, and it was found to be utterly impossible to turn the boat. To back out of the scrape was the only resort, and as soon as that could be effected it was done ; but not until the Allison had been twenty minutes under an exceedingly hot fire, in which she was repeatedly struck by shell and shot. She returned the fire from her thirty-pounder

Parrott gun forward, and occasioned the rebels considerable loss. The Allison was seriously damaged in the fray. The top of her pilot house was torn off, her smoke stack pierced by a shell, and her steam safety pipe cut away. It was a miracle she was not sunk. Finally extricating herself from her perilous position, also backed around the point of land and came to anchor with the rest of the flotilla, screened from the rebel battery by woods, but in short range. There they laid all night, prepared at any moment to repel any attempt on the part of the enemy to capture them by boarding. Several times during the night they fired upon the rebel reconnoitering parties, who became very bold in their advances.

All night long our men could hear the rattle of trains over the railroad, evidently conveying reinforcements to Kinston, against which General Foster had steadily pushed his advance, fighting for every inch of ground. The blows of axes, as the rebels felled trees to block up the avenues of approach to the town, the calls of soldiers, barking of dogs, and other sounds, were heard all the night long proceeding from the wooded shore. But no serious attempt was made to capture the boats, which might have been successful if well planned. On Sunday morning the boats turned, and descended the stream, as the water in the river had fallen nearly fifteen inches during the night, and promised to leave them high and dry, prizes to the rebels, if they much longer delayed their return. On their way down they were fired upon from the shores by guerrillas, who followed them a distance of twenty miles, killing one of our men (Edward J. Perkins, Company H, Marine Artillery), and wounding three others, none very seriously. The Ocean Wave, and, indeed, all the boats, were more or less injured by musketry and field pieces. Bullets were found on the Ocean Wave dipped in verdigris, to poison the wounds they inflicted, and others had copper wire attached, for the same purpose. The rebels evidently have been taking some new lessons in warfare from the Sepoys or Chinese; They are apt pupils. It would also appear that about 150 of these guerrillas were the attacking party, and thirty of them were killed and wounded before they relinquished the idea of taking the boats, as we have since learned. The attempt to pen in the boats, by felling trees across the river, was thwarted by the rapid movements of the boats.

On our return the Ocean Wave was unfortunate enough to stave a hole in her bottom by running on a stump, and sunk in three feet of water. She can be raised with but little trouble. Her guns have been taken off, as well as the crew, coal, provisions, etc., and she will soon be afloat. What effect this had on Gen. Foster's fortunes has not yet been ascertained. It probably prevented some rebel troops from meeting his forces.

If the river had been up, the flotilla would have been of great service in aiding in the capture of Kinston; but lack of water prevented it. Colonel Manchester and the officers and men of the Marine Artillery have earned a still higher reputation for their gallantry and indomitable perseverance on this expedition. They are a valuable arm of the service, and merit better treatment than they have received from the authorities. It seems about time to recognize them as a corps, now that they are performing all duties contemplated in their organization. Justice ought to be done them.

Commander Murray is displaying an immense deal of energy in conducting naval operations in North Carolina waters, and is greatly aiding General Foster in his operations.

LOSSES IN THE THREE BATTLES:

Those of Kinston, Whitehall and the Goldsboro Bridge consolidated.

Ninth New Jersey, Col. C. A. Heckmann, 2 killed, 32 wounded, 2 missing. Battle of Whitehall, 44 wounded. Battle of Goldsboro, 11 wounded.

Fifth Rhode Island, Capt. J. B. Arnold, 1 killed, 4 wounded.

Third New York Artillery, Capt J. J. Morrison, Battery B, 2 wounded. Capt. E. S. Jenney, Battery F, 2 wounded.

Twenty-fourth New York Independent Battery, 1 killed.

General Wessell's Brigade — Eighty-fifth New York, 3 wounded. Ninety-sixth New York, Col. Charles O. Gray, 1 killed, 6 wounded. Twenty-second New York, 2 killed, 16 wounded.

One Hundred and First Pennsylvania did not lose any in killed or wounded.

Eighty-fifth Pennsylvania, 9 wounded.

One Hundred and Third Pennsylvania. When this regiment went into action it had about 450 men, and after the action it was found that it had 14 killed and 58 wounded.

Casualties in Second Brigade, First Division, Department of North Carolina, Col. Thos. G. Stevenson commanding, at Kinston, Whitehall, Everettville, December 14, 16 and 17, 1862 :

Tenth Connecticut Volunteers, Lieut.-Col. Robert Leggett commanding, 11 killed, 86 wounded, of whom 10 have since died

Twenty-fourth Massachusetts Volunteers, Major Robert H. Stevenson commanding, 1 killed, 7 wounded.

Forty-fourth Regiment Massachusetts Volunteers, Col. Francis S. Lee commanding, 8 killed, 13 wounded.

Fifth Regiment Rhode Island Volunteers, Capt. Job Arnold commanding, 1 killed, 3 wounded.

Battery F, First Regiment Rhode Island State Artillery, Capt. James Belger, 1 killed, 8 wounded; 10 horses killed and wounded.

Report of the casualties in the Third (Col.

H. C. Lee's) Brigade. The expedition to Goldsboro:

Fifth Massachusetts Volunteers, Col. Geo. H. Pierson, 7 wounded.

Third Massachusetts Volunteers, Col. Silas P. Richmond, 2 wounded.

Twenty-seventh Massachusetts Regiment, Col. H. C. Lee, 3 wounded.

Forty-sixth Massachusetts Regiment, Col. George Bowler, 2 killed, 3 wounded.

List of killed and wounded in the First Brigade, first division, commanded by Colonel Amory:

Seventeenth Massachusetts Volunteers, 1 killed, 29 wounded.

Forty-fifth Massachusetts, Col. Chas. R. Codman, 6 killed, 38 wounded.

Twenty-third Massachusetts, 14 killed, 52 wounded.

Fifty-first Massachusetts, Col. Abram B. R. Sprague, 2 wounded.

Forty-third Massachusetts, Col. Chas. L. Holbrook, 2 killed, 1 wounded.

Artillery Brigade, Col. J. H. Ledlie, commanding, 2 staff wounded.

Battery B, Capt. James J. Morrison, 4 wounded.

Battery F, Capt. E. S. Jenney, 8 wounded.

Battery E, Lieut. G. E. Ashby, commanding, 3 wounded.

Battery I, Lieut. George W. Thomas, commanding, 1 killed.

Battery K, Capt. James K. Angel, 2 killed, 5 wounded.

Twenty-fourth Battery, Capt. J. E. Lee, 1 killed.

Casualties in Third New York Cavalry: Company A, Capt. W. S. Joy, 3 wounded; 7 horses killed.

Company B, Capt. John F. Marshall, 7 wounded; 10 horses killed.

Company E, Capt. F. Jacobs, Jr., 2 wounded.

Company K, Capt Geo. W. Cole, 2 wounded.

It is impossible to send the list of the missing, which may turn up in a day or two.

[New York Times, Sept. 3, 1874.]

MAJOR-GEN. JOHN G. FOSTER.

The death of this distinguished soldier and military engineer is announced. He died at his mother's residence at Nashua, N. H., at 1 o'clock yesterday morning, in the fifty-first year of his age. He graduated at West Point, July 1, 1846, being in the same class with Generals George B. McClellan and Stonewall Jackson. He served in the war with Mexico, 1847-48, attached to the Company of Sappers, Miners, and Pontoniers, and was engaged in the siege of Vera Cruz, battle of Cerro Gordo, and battles of Contreras and Churubusco, in which he distinguished himself. On the 20th of August, 1847, he was promoted Brevet First Lieutenant. He was severely wounded on the 8th of September, 1847, while leading the forlorn hope at the capture of Molino del Rey. For his gallant conduct on this occasion he was promoted Brevet Captain, and was placed, with full pay, for more than two years on the sick list of the army. When convalescent, he joined Gen. R. E. Lee at Baltimore as Assistant Engineer, and afterwards was on the Coast Survey. He was Assistant Professor of Engineering at West Point from January, 1855, to June, 1857, and Superintending Engineer of the survey of the site of the fort at Willett's Point, Long Island; of the preliminary operations for building a fort at Sandy Hook, N. J.; of building Fort Sumter, and repairs of Fort Moultrie, Charleston Harbor, South Carolina, from 1858 to 1861. On the 1st of July, 1860, he was promoted Captain, Corps of Engineers, for fourteen years' continuous service. During the rebellion of the seceding States he was Chief Engineer of the fortifications of Charleston Harbor, South Carolina. He was also engaged in defense of Fort Sumter from 27th of December, 1860, to April 14, 1861, when it was surrendered and evacuated. For the distinguished part taken by him in the transfer of the garrison of Fort Moultrie to Fort Sumter he was, on the 20th December, 1860, promoted Brevet Major. Soon after the surrender of Fort Sumter he was given the command of a brigade, as second to General Burnside on the North Carolina expedition, in which he again distinguished himself. He took by storm the central fortification on the Island of Roanoke, which soon led to the entire possession of the island. For these services he was promoted Brevet Lieutenant Colonel on the 8th February,

1862, and Brevet-Colonel on the 12th March, 1862, for gallant and meritorious services in the capture of New Berne, N. C. He was present at the bombardment of Fort Macon, which capitulated 26th April, 1862, and on July 1, 1862, when Gen. Burnside was ordered to join Gen. McClellan, he was left in command of the division, and subsequently of the whole department of Virginia and North Carolina, with his headquarters at Old Point Comfort. During this period he successfully conducted the expedition to burn the Goldsboro Railroad Bridge, (December, 1862), was engaged in the action of Southwest Creek, December 14, 1862; at the battle of Kinston the following day; two days afterward at the action of Whitehall, and on the 18th of December, 1862, at the action of Goldsboro Bridge. He repulsed the rebel attack on New Berne, March 14, 1863. At the time of the investment of Little Washington, on Tar River, he performed one of the most gallant deeds in the annals of the war, by running in a small steamer past the rebel batteries commanding the channel, for the purpose of hurrying forward reinforcements to relieve the little garrison. The daring act was not unobserved by the rebels, who sent a solid shot through the stateroom of the General, but as he happened to be on deck, he escaped harm, reached New Berne in safety, and accomplished his purpose.

On December 12, 1863, he relieved General Burnside and took command of the Army and Department of the Ohio, which he retained up to February 9, 1864, when he was obliged to relinquish the command in consequence of severe injuries from the fall of his horse. He was obliged to be removed to Baltimore for surgical assistance, and while yet on his crutches, he was, on the 26th of May, 1864, placed in command of the Department of the South, and met and aided General Sherman when he completed his march to the sea. He was in command of this department up to February 11, 1865, when he was again relieved for surgical treatment. He was promoted Brevet Brigadier-General on March 13, 1865, for gallant and meritorious services in the capture of Savannah, Ga., and on the same day Brevet Major-General for "meritorious services in the field during the Rebellion." He subsequently commanded the Department of Florida from August 7, 1865, to December 5, 1866, and was on temporary duty in the Engineer Bureau, Washington, from January to May, 1867. General Foster had been in ill-health for about a year, and his condition recently was such as to leave no hope of his recovery. He was a man of commanding presence, great executive ability, and undaunted courage, and was at all times very popular with those under his command. The funeral will take place at 10 o'clock, a. m., Saturday, with military honors. It is expected that a detachment of regulars from Fort Warren will attend the funeral.

At a meeting of the citizens of Nashua last night, to make arrangements for the funeral of General Foster on Saturday, a committee was appointed to co-operate with the City Government. The public buildings will be draped and business suspended. Invitations were sent to President Grant, the Secretary of War, Ex-Governor Allen, of New Hampshire, and other distinguished persons

[New York Herald, Sept. 6, 1874.]

OBSEQUIES OF GENERAL FOSTER.

IMPRESSIVE CEREMONIES AT NASHUA, N. H.

NASHUA, N. H., Sept. 5, 1874.

Since the obsequies of Major Ainsworth, a Nashua man who fell at the head of his command at Front Royal, there has not been so profound an expression of sorrow as that evinced in this city to-day, over the death and funeral rites of her honored citizen, patriot and gallant soldier of two wars, Major-General John G. Foster. The morning dawned foggy and heavy, but mellowed into autumnal splendor, while the populace seemed subdued in thought and mindful that one was being consigned to mother earth who had performed his duty to his country wisely and well. The mills and workshops, stores and offices were closed, and the citizens and citizen-soldiers of Nashua and vicinity vied with one another in paying the last sad tribute of respect to a son of New Hampshire who has honored her on many fields of carnage, and whose name is a household word with her children.

At 8 o'clock a requiem mass was held at the Church of the Immaculate Conception by Rev. John O'Donnell, and at the same hour a detail of ten men from Post John G. Foster, under command of Colonel George Bowers, took charge of the remains at the residence of his mother on Orange square, where the body laid in state two hours. Lighted candles were burning at the head and feet, according to the custom of the Catholic Church. .

The body was encased in a heavy rosewood casket, upon which lay the sword, sash and belt of the deceased soldier. On the inner side of the lid, which was turned back, was a large floral wreath about a heavy silver coffin plate, upon which were handsomely engraved emblems of the army and the following inscription:—"John Gray Foster, Lieutenant-Colonel Engineers, Brevet Major-General United States Army, died September 2, 1874, aged 51 years." Hundreds of citizens, women and children viewed the remains, and hundreds more, owing to the crowd, were unable to look upon the face of the dead, which, although emaciated by disease, bore the soldierly impress it was wont to bear in life. The arrangements at the house were under the direction of Captain Solomon Spalding.

The city flags were at half-mast, minute guns were fired from 10 until 12 o'clock, and all the bells in the city were tolled. The cortege received the remains at his mother's residence and proceeded to the Church of the Immaculate Conception, the nave of which was heavily draped in mourning, via. Orange, Concord, Main, East Pearl and Temple streets, where the body was placed in front of the altar, and the funeral service of the Catholic Church was performed by the Right Rev. Bishop Lynch, of South Carolina. The funeral oration was delivered by Rev. Robert Fulton, S. J., and President of the Boston College, connected with the Church of the Immaculate Conception, of which the deceased soldier was a member.

The singing, which was grand and appropriate, was by the choir of the Church of St. Aloysius, assisted by General Michael T. Donahue and others, from Boston, and John McEvoy, of Lowell.

At the close of the exercises in the church the procession was re-formed, when it proceeded through Amory street to Canal street, up Canal street to the Nashua Cemetery, in the rear of the Unitarian church, where the remains of the gallant dead were interred with those of his kindred, and the grave blessed by Rev. Father O'Donnell.

The following regiments participated in these battles:

Third Regiment Massachusetts Volunteer Militia, Col. S. P. Richmond.

Fifth Regiment Massachusetts Volunteer Militia, Col. Geo. H. Pierson.

*Eighth Regiment Massachusetts Volunteer Militia, Col. F. J. Coffin.

Seventeenth Regiment Massachusetts Volunteer Infantry, Col. T. J. C. Amory.

Twenty-third Regiment Massachusetts Volunteer Infantry, Major J. G. Chambers.

Twenty-fourth Regiment Massachusetts Volunteer Infantry, Col. T. G. Stevenson.

Twenty-fifth Regiment Massachusetts Volunteer Infantry, Col. Josiah Picket.

Twenty-seventh Regiment Massachusetts Volunteer Infantry, Col. H. C. Lee.

Forty-third Regiment Massachusetts Volunteer Militia, Col. Chas. L. Holbrook.

---

*Eighth Massachusetts Regiment garrison New Berne while the other troops were away.

Forty-fourth Regiment Massachusetts Volunteer Militia, Col. Francis S. Lee.

Forty-fifth Regiment Massachusetts Volunteer Militia, Col. Chas. R. Codman.

Forty-sixth Regiment Massachusetts Volunteer Militia, Col. Geo. Bowler.

Fifty-first Regiment Massachusetts Volunteer Militia, Col. A. B. R. Sprague.

Battery F, First Regiment Rhode Island, Capt. James Belger.

Fifth Regiment Rhode Island Volunteers, Capt Job Arnold.

Third Regiment Cavalry, New York State Volunteers, Col. S. H. Mix. Company A, Capt. Walter S. Joy; Company B, Capt. John F. Marshall; Company E, Capt. Ferrish Jacobs, Jr.; Company K, Capt. George W. Cole.

Third New York Artillery, State Volunteers, Col. J. H. Ledlie. Battery B, Capt. Joseph J. Morrison; Battery C, Lieut. G. E. Ashby; Battery F, Capt. E. S. Jenney;

Battery I, Capt. John H. Ammon; Battery K, Capt. James R. Angel.

Twenty-second New York Infantry, State Volunteers, Col. Walter Phelps, Jr.

Eighty-fifth New York Infantry, State Volunteers, Col J. S. Belknap.

Ninety-sixth New York Infantry, State Volunteers, Col. Chas. O. Gray.

Tenth Connecticut Volunteers, Col. E. D. S. Goodyear.

Twenty-fourth Independent Battery, New York State Volunteers, Capt. T. E. Lee.

Ninth Regiment New Jersey Infantry, Col. C. A. Heckmann.

Eighty-fifth Regiment Pennsylvania.

One Hundred and First Regiment Pennsylvania.

One Hundred and Third Regiment Pennsylvania.

INDEX.

Ainsworth, Major	86
Allen, Ex-Gov.	86
Allison	60, 72, 73
Allis' Flying Artillery . .	17, 32, 42
Ammon, Captain John H. . .	44, 91
Ammon's Battery	44
Amory, Colonel Thomas J. C. . .	80, 90
Amory's Brigade . . .	50, 55, 80
Angel, Captain James R. . . .	81, 91
Angel's Battery	42
Ashby, Lieut. G. E.	81
Arnold, Job Col. B.	78, 79
Atlantic and North Carolina R. R. . .	58
Ball's Bluff	54, 59
Baltimore, Md.	85
Belger's Battery F, First Rhode Island Artil'y	39, 51, 66, 79, 90
Belger, Captain James, . . .	44, 79
Belknap, Col. J. L.	91
Black Pioneer Brigade	12
Boston, Mass.	89
Boston College	88
Bowler, Col. George	80, 91

Index.

Bowers, Col, George	87
Butler, Henry	26
Butler, Aug. G.	11
Bradford, J. A.	22
Burnside, Gen. A. E.	83
Catholic Church	88, 89
Cerro Gordo	82
Chambers, Major John G.	57, 89
Chapman, Franklin	13
Chapman, —— wounded	63
Charleston Harbor, S. C.	83
Cherebusco	82
Chinese	76
Church of the Immaculate Conception	87, 89
Church of St. Aloysius	89
Clifford	1
Codman, Col. C. R.	80, 91
Coffin, Col. F. T.	90
Cole, Capt. Geo. W.	11, 13, 21, 61, 62, 65, 68, 69, 70, 81, 91
Company B, Third New York Cavalry	10, 61, 91
Company K, Third New York Cavalry	10, 13, 22, 61, 65, 68, 70, 80, 91
Company K, Ninth New Jersey	63
Company K, Ninety-sixth New York	67
Confederate States	45
Connecticut Tenth Infantry	18, 21, 57, 71, 78, 92
Contreras	82

Costello, John, wounded . . . 11, 62
Day, Lieut. S. S. 12
Department of Florida 85
Department of the South 85
Dublin County, North Carolina . . 45
Dudley Station, N. C. 41
Donahue, Gen. M. T. 89
Eighth Massachusetts Infantry . . 90, 91
Eighteenth South Carolina Regiment . 16
Eighty-fifth New York Infantry, . 78, 92
Eighty-eighth New York Infantry . 15, 91
Eighty-fifth Pennsylvania . 14, 15, 78, 92
Ellis, John W. 46
Evans, Maj.-Gen. N. S. 17, 19, 20, 22, 24, 54, 56, 59
Evansville, N. C. 79
Everett Station 41
Fellows, Lieut.-Col. John F. . . . 36
Fifth Massachusetts Infantry , . 80, 90
Fifty-first Massachusetts Infantry . 80, 91
Fifth Rhode Island Infantry . . 79, 91
Fitzsimmons, Major Chas. . . . 41
Florida, Department of 85
Forty-sixth Regiment Massachusetts Volunteer
 Infantry 58, 80, 91
Forty-third Regiment Massachusetts Volunteer
 Militia Infantry . . . 42, 80, 90
Forty-fourth Regiment Massachusetts Volunteer
 Militia Infantry 55, 79, 91

Forth-fifth Regiment Massachusetts Volunteer
   Militia Infantry . . 15, 16, 55, 80, 91
Foster, Maj.-Gen. John G. 9, 19, 20, 21, 29, 30, 34,
   37, 38, 42, 48, 50, 58, 60, 66, 68, 70, 71, 72, 74,
                                  76, 77, 82, 86, 87, 88
Foster, Maj.-Gen. John G., Obsequies of . 86
Foster, Maj.-Gen. John G., Post . 87
Franklin, N. C. 39
Franklin, Major 18, 19
Front Royal 86
Fulton, Rev. Robert 88
Garrard, Major Jeptha 17, 24, 28, 29, 31, 41, 42
Georgia 71
Georgia, Savannah 85
Goldsboro 19, 22, 27, 32, 33, 40, 44, 49, 56, 58,
                                            59, 77
Goldsboro R. R. Bridge . . . 48, 77, 84
Goldsboro and Wilmington R. R. . 32, 41
Grant, President U. S. 86
Gray, Col. Charles O. . 20, 67, 70, 78, 92
Gray, Col. Chas. O., Death of . . 57, 67
Graham, Lieut. Geo. W. 38
Gunboats :
    Delaware 71
    Seymour 71
    Shawsheen 71
Harper Bros. 5
Harper's History of the Rebellion . . 5

Index. v

Heckmann, Col. C. A.	10, 13, 21, 37, 62, 63, 65, 66, 78, 92
Holbrook, Col. Chas. L.	13, 42, 80, 90
Hunt, Col. Lewis C.	21
Jacobs, Jr., Capt. Ferris	17, 32, 33, 41, 91
Jackson, Gen. Stonewall	82
Jenney, Capt. E. S.	15, 24, 78, 81, 91
Jerseymen	64
Joy, Capt. Walter S.	81
Kennedy, Major T. D.	44
Kingsley, Franklin	11
Kinston, N. C.	9, 14, 18, 23, 24, 27, 46, 48, 49, 51, 53, 55, 56, 58, 59, 60, 61, 65, 67, 68, 72, 73, 74, 77, 84
Ledlie, Col. J. H.	21, 30, 50, 81, 91
Lee's Brigade	39, 50, 55
Lee, Col. Francis S.	79, 91
Lee, Col. H. C.	80, 90
Lee, Capt. O. E.	92
Lee, Gen. R. E.	82
Leggett, Lieut-Col.	79, 91
Lemon, Wm.	38
Little Washington, N. C.	70, 84
Lincoln, Abraham	45
Lowell, Mass.	89
Lynch, Rev. Bishop	88
Macon, Fort, S. C.	84
Manchester, Lieut.-Col. H. A.	17, 60, 72, 77

Marine Artillery, New York . . 72, 75 77
Marshall, Capt. James F. . . 10, 61, 81, 91
Massachusetts 29, 30
" Third Regiment Vol. M. 80, 90
" Fifth Regiment Vol. M. 80, 90
" Eighth Regiment Vol. M. 89, 90
" Seventeenth Regiment Inf. 16, 36, 37, 38, 80, 90
" Twenty-third Regiment Inf. 16, 54, 57, 80, 90
" Twenty-fourth Regiment Inf. 79, 90
" Twenty-fifth Regiment Inf. 90
" Twenty-seventh Regiment Inf. 80, 90
" Forty-third Regiment Vol. M. 42, 80, 90
" Forty-fourth Regiment Vol. M. 55, 79, 91
" Forty-fifth Regiment Vol. M. 15, 16, 55, 80, 91
" Forty-sixth Regiment Vol. M. 58, 80, 91
" Fifty-first Regiment Vol. M. 80, 91
McClellan, Gen. George B. . . . 82
McEvoy, John 89
Merrimac 27

Mexico	82
Mexico, Molino del Rey	82
Mix's Cavalry	51, 53
Mix, Col. Simon H.	51, 59, 90
Mix, Lieut. John	12, 51
Mollett, Col.	16
Morrison, Capt. Joseph J.	13, 44, 50, 52, 78, 81, 91
Morrison's Battery	12, 13, 14, 39, 44, 48, 52
Mosely Hall, N. C.	27
Moultrie, Fort, S. C.	83
Mount Olive Station, N. C.	29, 31, 32, 33, 34, 44
Murray, Capt.	17
Murray, Commander A.	71, 72, 77
Nashua, N. H.	82, 86, 89
Nethercote, Major	16
Nethercote's N. C. Battalion	16, 61
Neucommer, ——	14, 70
Neuse River Bridge	66
Neuse River	16, 23, 27, 41, 42, 56, 59
New Berne	9, 47, 58, 60, 62, 67, 70, 71, 83, 84
New Hampshire	86, 87

New York Third Artillery:—

A	43
B	43, 50, 58, 60, 77, 80, 91
C	43, 91
D	43
E	43, 80, 81, 91
F	43, 77, 91

New York Third Artillery, continued.

H	43
I	43, 80, 92
K	43, 80, 81, 92

New York Third Artillery	12, 13, 14, 18, 24, 43, 44, 50, 66, 77
New York Third Cavalry	9, 10, 11, 12, 13, 17, 22, 24, 26, 32, 41, 43, 51, 57, 59, 80, 91
A	46, 91
B	10, 91
C	26
D	43, 46
E	91
G	43, 46
K	10, 13, 22, 58, 61, 68, 69, 91
New York Eighty-eighth Infantry	15
" Ninety-second Infantry	15
" Ninety-sixth Infantry	15, 57, 67, 70, 78
New York Herald	5, 86
New York Times	5, 81
New Yorkers	59
New York	1, 5
Nicolo, ——	23
Ninth New Jersey	10, 12, 13, 14, 15, 18, 21, 28, 29, 36, 37, 43, 50, 52, 53, 54, 55, 62, 63, 64, 68, 70, 71, 78, 92
North Carolinians	59
North Carolina	1, 33, 45, 54, 77, 78, 83, 92

Index.   ix

North Carolina Infantry	16
" " Second Cavalry	59
" " Third Cavalry	16
" " Rebel Troops	60
Ocean Wave, Gunboat	60, 75, 76
O'Donnell, Rev. John	87, 89
Ohio, Department of	85
Old Point Comfort, Va.	84
One Hundred and First Pennsylvania	15, 78, 92
One Hundeed and Third Pennsylvania	15, 78, 92
Parrott Gun	74
Peck's, Gen., Brigade	50
Perkins, Edward J., Death of	75
Perkins, Lieut. W. W., Death of	57
Pennsylvania Eighty-fifth Regiment	15, 78, 92
Pennsylvania One Hundred and First	15, 78, 92
Pennsylvania One Hundred and Third	15, 78, 92
Pettigrew, Gen. J. J.	37
Phelps, Col. Walter, Jr.	92
Pickett, Col. Josiah	90
Pierson, Col. George N.	79, 90
Pioneers, Contraband	10
Poisoned Bullets	75
Pond, Capt. N. P.	32
Porter, Col.	19
Provost-Marshall, Major Franklin	18
Ransom's Twenty-third N. Y. Artillery	41
Richmond, Col. S. P.	80, 90

Index.

Rhode Island Fifth Regiment Infantry	91
Riggs', William J., Battery	44
Raleigh, N. C.	16
Roanoke Island, N. C.	83
Rocket Battery	38
Rogers, ———	22
Rodman Gun	13
Sandy Hook, N. J.	83
Savannah, Ga.	85
Schenck, Capt. Theo. H., Battery	62, 66
Second N. C. Cavalry	59
Seventeenth Infantry, Massachusetts Volunteers	16, 36, 37, 38, 80, 90
Sepoys	76
Sherman, Gen. W. T.	85
Sleight, Capt. J. C.	41
Snow Hill, N. C.	57
South Carolina Regiments	39, 44, 48, 54, 56, 57
South Carolina Second Cavalry	16
" " Seventeenth Infantry	16
" " Eighteenth Infantry	16
" " Twenty-third Infantry	16
Southwest Creek, N. C.	11, 61, 84
Spalding, Capt. S.	88
Sprague, Col. A. B. R.	80, 91
Steamboats :—	
Ocean Wave	60, 71, 76
Allison	60, 72, 73

Steamboats, continued.
   North State 71
   Port Royal 71
   Wilson 71
Stevenson's Brigade 50, 55
Stevenson, Thomas G. Col. . . 79, 90
Stevenson, Major R. N. 79
Suffolk, Virginia 50
Sumter, Fort, S. C. 82, 83
Tar River 84
Tenth Conn. Volunteer Inf. 18, 21, 51, 71, 79, 92
Third Massachusetts Volunteers . 80, 90
Third New York Artillery 12, 13, 14, 18, 24, 43, 44, 50, 66, 77
Third New York Cavalry 9, 10, 11, 12, 13, 17, 22, 24, 26, 32, 41, 43, 51, 57, 59, 80, 91
Third New York Cavalry:—
   Company A 46, 91
         B 10, 91
         D 26, 43
         E 91
         G 43, 46
         K . 10, 13, 22, 58, 61, 68, 69, 91
Trenton, N. C. . . . .
Trent Road 50
Trent River 50
Twenty-third Infantry, Massachusetts Volunteers 16, 54, 57, 80, 90

Index.

Twenty-fifth Massachusetts Volunteers	90
Twenty.fourth Massachusetts Volunteers	79, 90
Twenty-seventh Massachusets Volunteer Inf.	80, 90
Twenty-third New York Independent Battery	44
Twenty-fourth New York Independent Battery	44, 77, 80, 92
Union Troops	58, 59
United States Navy	71
Vera Cruz	81
Washington, D. C.	85
Wayne County, N. C.	45, 56
Weldon, N. C.	49
Wells, Capt. Henry A., Death of	57
Wessell's Brigade	13, 15, 29, 50, 53, 54, 55, 78
Wessell, Gen. H. W.	15, 59, 65
West Point	83
Whitehall, N. C.	1, 5, 9, 24, 28, 29, 30, 31, 40, 43, 52, 77, 84
Whitfield, Capt.	50
Willett's Point, Long Island	82
Wilmington and Weldon R. R.	49, 58
Wilmington, N. C..	31, 32, 40
Wilson, Capt. John M.	32
Wilson, Henry W.	10

www.ingramcontent.com/pod-product-compliance
Lightning Source LLC
Chambersburg PA
CBHW021946160426
43195CB00011B/1245